Janice VanCleave's
ELECTRICITY

JANICE VANCLEAVE'S
SPECTACULAR SCIENCE PROJECTS

Animals
Earthquakes
Electricity
Gravity
Machines
Magnets
Microscopes and Magnifying Lenses
Molecules
Volcanoes

JANICE VANCLEAVE'S
SCIENCE FOR EVERY KID SERIES

Astronomy for Every Kid
Biology for Every Kid
Chemistry for Every Kid
Dinosaurs for Every Kid
Earth Science for Every Kid
Geography for Every Kid
Math for Every Kid
Physics for Every Kid

Spectacular Science Projects

Janice VanCleave's

ELECTRICITY

Mind-boggling Experiments You Can Turn Into Science Fair Projects

John Wiley & Sons, Inc.
New York • Chichester • Brisbane • Toronto • Singapore

Design and Production by Navta Associates, Inc.
Illustrated by Doris Ettlinger

Library of Congress Cataloging-in-Publication Data
VanCleave, Janice.
 [Electricity]
 Janice VanCleave's electricity: mind-boggling experiments you can turn into science fair projects / Janice VanCleave.
 p.   cm.
 Includes index.
 ISBN 0-471-31010-7
 1. Electricity—Experiments—Juvenile literature. 2. Science projects—Juvenile literature. [1. Electricity—Experiments. 2. Experiments. 3. Science Projects.] I. Title.
 QC527.2.V36   1994
 537'.078–dc20   93-40913

Printed in the United States of America
10 9 8 7 5 4 3 2 1

CONTENTS

Introduction	1
1. Wanderer	4
2. Movers	8
3. Stickers	12
4. Zap!	16
5. Glow Bulb	20
6. Charger	24
7. How High?	28
8. Flow Rate	32
9. Pathway	36
10. Lemon Power	40
11. Give and Take	44
12. Flashlight	48
13. Series	52
14. Parallel	56
15. Resistance	60
16. Protectors	64
17. Attractive	68
18. Pointer	72
19. Jerker	76
20. Generator	80
Appendix	84
Glossary	85
Index	88

This book is dedicated to a special person who started my writing career and periodically gives it an extra charge,

Mary Kennan Herbert

Introduction

Science is a search for answers. Science projects are good ways to learn more about science as you search for the answers to specific problems. This book will give you guidance and provide ideas, but you must do your part in the search by planning experiments, finding and recording information related to the problem, and organizing the data collected to find the answer to the problem. Sharing your findings by presenting your project at science fairs will be a rewarding experience if you have properly prepared for the exhibit. Trying to assemble a project overnight results in frustration, and you cheat yourself out of the fun of being a science detective. Solving a scientific mystery, like solving a detective mystery, requires planning and the careful collecting of facts. The following sections provide suggestions for how to get started on this scientific quest. Start the project with curiosity and a desire to learn something new.

SELECT A TOPIC

The 20 topics in this book suggest many possible problems to solve. Each topic has one "cookbook" experiment—follow the recipe and the result is guaranteed. Approximate metric equivalents have been given after all English measurements. Try several or all of these easy experiments before choosing the topic you like best and want to know more about. Regardless of the problem you choose to solve, what you discover will make you more knowledgeable about electricity.

KEEP A JOURNAL

Purchase a bound notebook in which you will write everything relating to the project. This is your journal. It will contain your original ideas as well as ideas you get from books or from people like teachers and scientists. It will include descriptions of your experiments as well as diagrams, photographs, and written observations of all your results. Every entry should be as neat as possible and dated. Information from this journal can be used to write a report of your project, and you will want to display the journal with your completed project. A neat, orderly journal provides a complete and accurate record of your project from start to finish. It is also proof of the time you spent sleuthing out the answers to the scientific mystery you undertook to solve.

LET'S EXPLORE

This section of each chapter follows each of 20 sample experiments and provides additional questions about the problem presented in the experiment. By making small changes to some part of the sample experiment, new results are achieved. Think about why these new results might have happened.

SHOW TIME!

You can use the format of the sample experiment to design your own experiments to solve the questions asked in "Let's Explore." Your own experiment should follow the sample experiment's format and include a single question about one idea, a list of necessary materials, a detailed step-by-step procedure, written results with diagrams, graphs, and charts if they seem helpful, and a conclusion answering and explaining the question. Include any information you found through research to clarify your answer. When you design your own experiments, make sure to get adult approval if supplies or procedures other than those given in this book are used.

WARNING: Use only the indicated number and size of batteries to perform the experiments. Never use the main electricity supply—it can produce a shock that can kill you. Never use old batteries or try to take a battery apart.

If you want to make a science fair project, study the information listed here and after each sample experiment in the book to develop your ideas into a real science fair exhibit. Use the suggestions that best apply to the project topic that you have chosen. Keep in mind that while your display represents all the work that you have done, it must tell the story of the project in such a way that it attracts and holds the interest of the viewer. So keep it simple. Do not try to cram all of your information into one place. To have more space on the display and still exhibit all your work, keep some of the charts, graphs, pictures, and other materials in your journal instead of on the display board itself.

The actual size and shape of displays can be different, depending on the local science fair officials, so you will have to check the rules for your science fair. Most exhibits are allowed to be 48 inches (122 cm) wide, 30 inches (76 cm) deep, and 108 inches (274 cm) high. These are maximum measurements and your display may be smaller than this. A three-sided backboard (see drawing) is usually the best way to display your work. Wooden panels can be hinged together, but you can also use sturdy cardboard pieces taped together to form a very inexpensive but presentable exhibit.

A good title of six words or less with a maximum of 50 characters should be placed at the top of the center panel. The title should capture the theme of the project but should not be the same as the problem statement. For example, if the problem under question is *What is electricity?*, a good title of the project may be "Moving Electrons." The title and other headings should be neat and large enough to be readable at a distance of

about 3 feet (1 meter). [...] an glue letters to the backboard (y[...] use precut letters that you buy or let[...]t you cut out of construction pape[...] you can stencil the letters for all the[...] A short summary paragraph of abo[...] words to explain the scientific principles involved is good and can be printed under the title. A person who has no knowledge of the topic should be able to easily understand the basic idea of the project just from reading the summary.

There are no set rules about the position of the information on the display. However, it all needs to be well organized, with the title and summary paragraph as the main point at the top of the center and the remaining material placed neatly from left to right under specific headings. Choices of headings will depend on how you wish to display the information. Separate headings for Problem, Procedure, Results, and Conclusion may be used.

The judges give points for how clearly you are able to discuss the project and explain its purpose, procedure, results, and conclusion. The display should be organized so that it explains everything, but your ability to discuss your project and answer the questions of the judges convinces them that you did the work and understand what you have done. Practice a speech in front of friends, and invite them to ask you questions. If you do not know the answer to a question, never guess or make up an answer or just say, "I do not know." Instead, you can say that you did not discover that answer during your research and then offer other information that you found of interest about the project. Be proud of the project and approach the judges with enthusiasm about your work.

CHECK IT OUT!

Read about your topic in many books and magazines. You are more likely to have a successful project if you are well informed about the topic. For the topics in this book, some tips are provided about specific places to look for information. Record in your journal all the information you find, and include for each source the author's name, the book title (or magazine name and article title), the numbers of the pages you read, the publisher's name, where it was published, and the year of publication.

Wanderer

PROBLEM

How does matter become electrically charged?

Materials

masking tape
2 rulers
12-inch (30-cm) piece of string
scissors
sheet black construction paper, 12
   inches × 16 inches (30 cm × 45 cm)
marking pen
6 round labels with ⅜-inch (.95 cm)
   diameters, 2 different colors with 3
   labels in each set

Procedure

1. Tape one ruler to a table, with about 2 inches (5 cm) extending over the edge.

2. Tape one end of the string to the end of the ruler that is hanging over the table's edge.

3. Cut a circle with a 2-inch (5-cm) **diameter** (the measure of a line crossing a circle and passing through the circle's center point) from the black paper.

4. Tape the free end of the string to the edge of the paper circle.

5. Cut two 1-inch (2.5-cm) wide rings from the black paper. Make the diameter of one ring 6 inches (15 cm) and the diameter of the other ring 10 inches (25 cm).

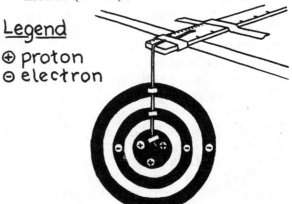

Legend
⊕ proton
⊖ electron

6. Tape the rings to the string so that they are evenly spaced, with the paper circle hanging in the center of the rings.

7. Write a positive sign (+) on one set of three colored labels, and a negative sign (–) on the second set.

8. Affix all the labels with a positive sign on the paper circle, at random.

9. Place two labels with a negative sign on the inner ring and the remaining negative label on the outer ring, as in the diagram on page 4.

Results

You have constructed a model of a lithium atom showing its electrical charges.

Why?

There are only two known types of **electric charges**, positive and negative. A **proton** has a positive charge of +1, and an **electron** has a negative charge of –1. Protons are found in the **nucleus** (center) of atoms, and electrons spin around the outside of the nucleus. **Matter** is anything that takes up space and has mass, such as gases, liquids, and solids. All matter is made up of **atoms**, which are the smallest part of an element that retains the properties of the element.

Lithium is one type of atom. The symbol for Lithium is Li. Lithium atoms, like all atoms, are **electrically neutral**. This means that the number of positive charges (protons) in the atom equals the number of negative charges (electrons). Electrons move in and out of fixed pathways outside the nucleus. These paths are represented by the "rings" in the lithium model. The "rings" vary in distance from the nucleus and are not confined pathways. They just indicate areas where electrons are most likely to be found.

LET'S EXPLORE

1. What happens if the number of electrons in the electrically neutral lithium atom changes? A decrease or increase in the number of electrons changes any atom into an **ion** (a charged particle). Some atoms, such as Lithium, tend to lose electrons. The electrons in the outermost part of the atom are held more loosely, and it is these electrons that are usually lost. When an

atom loses an electron, the remaining number of electrons is less than the number of protons, and the atom becomes a positively-charged ion called a **cation**. Produce a model of a cation by repeating the activity using 1 less electron in the outer ring.

ions to prepare a poster showing the gain and loss of electrons in the formation of ions.

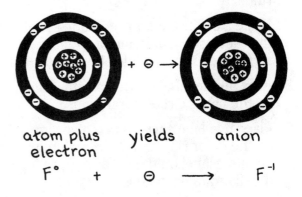

atom plus electron   yields   anion

$F°$ $+$ $\ominus$ $\longrightarrow$ F^{-1}

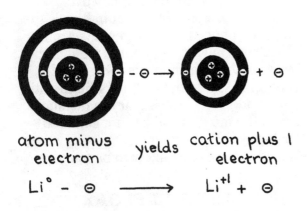

atom minus electron   yields   cation plus 1 electron

$Li°$ $-$ $\ominus$ $\longrightarrow$ Li^{+1} $+$ $\ominus$

SHOW TIME!

2. Atoms, such as Flourine, that tend to gain electrons take on a negative charge and are called **anions**. Prepare a model of an anion by using the procedure in the original activity, using 9 protons and 9 electrons in the atom, and add an extra electron to the outer ring for the anion. **Science Fair Hint:** Use models of the atoms and

1. Another example of electron movement is when a rod made up of carbon atoms is rubbed by a material such as a cloth. If the carbon electrons are more easily lost than those in the atoms of the cloth, the electrons are transferred from the rod to the cloth, making the rubbed surface of the rod positively-charged and that of the cloth negatively charged. Use a diagram to show the results of this type of electron motion.

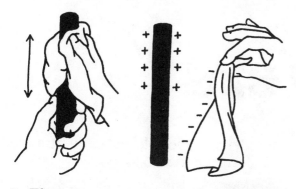

2. Electrons can manage to break away from atoms but wander around among the surrounding atoms within the material. These electrons are called **"free" electrons**. It is the movement of these free electrons that produces an **electric current** (a flow of electric charges). As the number of free electrons increases in a material, it becomes more capable of conducting an electric current and is called an **electrical conductor**.

Free electrons do not flow instantly from one end of an electrical wire to the other like water running swiftly through a pipe. Rather, they move forward and bump into other free electrons, sending them forward; thus, there is a slow drift of electrons through the wire, but a speedy transfer of energy from one electron to the next. This movement of electrons and transfer of energy, called an **electrical impulse**, can be demonstrated. Have 10 or more people, including yourself, stand in a line one arm's length apart in a circle. Each person's palm should be about 1 inch (2.5 cm) from the back of the person in front of them. You will begin by moving forward just enough to press your hand against the back of the person in front of you. Instruct each person that after being touched, they are to move forward and gently press their hand against the back of the person in front of them. Stop the experiment when you are touched. This experiment simulates the slow forward speed of free electrons, which is about 0.0001 yards (0.0001 m) per second, and the speed of the transfer of electrical impulses from one electron to the next, which is 300,000,000 yards (300,000,000 m) per second. In the time it took for the impulse (hand touching the back) to travel the distance around the circle the electrons (people in circle) only slightly moved forward one step.

2

Movers

PROBLEM

How does electricity produce movement?

Materials

modeling clay
flexible plastic drinking straw
ruler
scissors
tissue paper
cellophane tape
transparent plastic report folder
sheet of typing paper

Procedure

NOTE: This activity works best when the air is cold and dry.

1. Press a walnut-sized piece of clay onto a table top.

2. Insert the inflexible end of the straw into the clay.

3. Bend the flexible end of the straw to form a horizontal arm.

4. Measure and cut a 1-inch × 8-inch (2.5-cm × 20-cm) strip from the tissue paper.

5. Bend the paper strip in half and hang it on the horizontal arm of the straw. The hanging ends of the paper will be called "leaves."

6. Use a small piece of tape to secure the top of the paper strip to the straw's arm.

7. Cut a 4-inch (10-cm) square from the plastic folder.

8. Lay the sheet of typing paper on the table, and rub the square of plastic back and forth across the paper five or six times.

9. Hold the plastic square close to one of the paper leaves, and touch the plastic to the leaf.

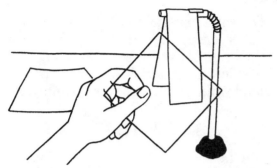

10. Repeat the procedure, touching the plastic to the second leaf.

11. Rub the plastic on the paper again. Holding it perpendicular to the table, insert it between the two paper leaves.

Results

At first the paper leaves move toward the plastic sheet, but after being touched by the plastic they move away from each other and from the plastic sheet.

Why?

Electricity is a form of energy associated with the presence and movement of electrical charges. The two known types of electrical charges are positive and negative. Atoms, such as those in paper and plastic, contain positively-charged protons in their nucleus and negatively-charged electrons outside the nucleus. The plastic will become negatively charged if the electrons are rubbed off the atoms of paper and collect on the plastic. The paper that forms the leaves is electrically neutral until the charged plastic is moved close to them. The **law of electric charges** states that unlike charges attract each other and like charges **repel** (push apart from) each other. The negatively-charged electrons in the electrically neutral paper are repelled by the negatively-charged plastic. This results in an excess of positive charges on the paper's surface closest to the plastic. The attraction between the unlike charges—the positive charges on the paper and the negative charges on the plastic—is great enough to overcome the downward pull of gravity and move the paper toward the plastic.

Touching the leaves with the plastic allows electrons to be transferred to the leaves, giving the leaves a negative charge like that of the plastic sheet. Again, the law for electric charges states that like charges repel each other. The negative charge on the leaves results in the leaves pushing away from each other as well as from the negatively-charged plastic sheet. The force of attraction or repulsion between electrical charges is called an **electrostatic force**.

LET'S EXPLORE

1. Would the width of the paper leaves affect the results? Repeat the experiment twice, first using a strip of paper less than 1 inch (2.5 cm) wide, and then using a strip wider than 1 inch (2.5 cm).

2. Does the material used to charge the paper leaves affect the results? Repeat the original experiment, replacing the plastic with materials such as plastic food wrap, wool, wax paper, and nylon.

SHOW TIME!

1. Further demonstrate the laws of electric charges by repeating the original experiment using two straws and two strips of paper. Place the straws about

2 inches (5 cm) apart. Design methods of charging the paper leaves so that you can determine:

- how to show opposite charges attracting.
- how to show attraction between a charged object and an uncharged object.
- how to distinguish attraction of opposite-charged objects from attraction between a charged and an uncharged object.
- how to show repulsion of like charges.

Use diagrams to record and display your results.

2. Another way of demonstrating the laws of electric charges is by making two hanging metal balls. Each hanging ball is made by wadding a 2-inch × 2-inch (5-cm × 5-cm) piece of aluminum foil around the end of a 12-inch (30-cm) single strand of thread. Tape the ends of the threads on the

edge of a table so that the balls are as close as possible without touching. Follow the procedure in the original experiment to charge the metal balls.

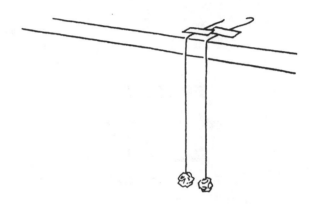

CHECK IT OUT!

Electric charges are more likely to collect on materials if the air is cool and dry. Use a physical science book to find out how the temperature of the air and its moisture content, called humidity, affect the build-up of electric charges.

3

Stickers

PROBLEM

How is static electricity produced?

Materials

9-inch (23-cm) round balloon
ruler
scissors
sewing thread
masking tape
hand soap
water
towel
adult helper and a hair dryer if the air
   is humid

Procedure

NOTE: This experiment works best on a dry day. If the air is very humid, ask an adult to dry the balloon with a hair dryer.

1. Inflate the balloon and knot the end.

2. Tie a 12-inch (30-cm) piece of thread to the balloon.

3. Tape the free end of the string to the edge of a table.

4. Wash and dry your hands. Your hands must be clean and very dry.

5. Sit on the floor near the balloon.

6. Hold the balloon in one hand and quickly rub the other hand back and forth across the surface of the balloon eight to ten times.

7. Release the balloon and allow it to hang freely.

8. Hold the hand rubbed against the balloon near and to the side of, but not touching, the balloon.

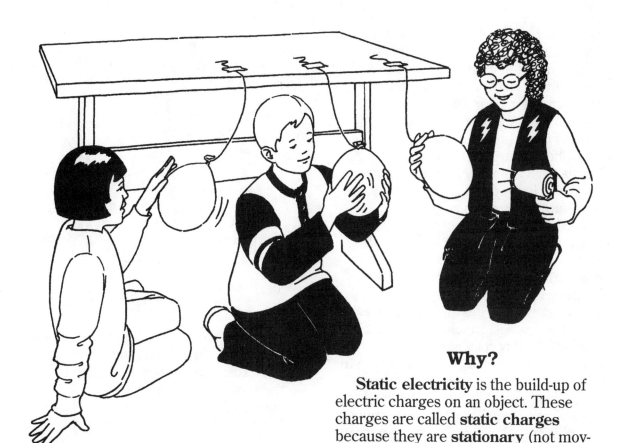

Why?

Static electricity is the build-up of electric charges on an object. These charges are called **static charges** because they are **stationary** (not moving). These static charges can be positive or negative. All substances are made up of atoms. Every atom has a nucleus containing protons and electrons spinning around it. The protons have a positive electrical charge, and the electrons have

Results

The balloon moves toward your hand. The balloon actually moves upward through the air to reach your hand.

a negative charge. When two substances such as the balloon and your hand are rubbed together, electrons are pulled over from the material that has the weaker attraction for them (the hand) and attach to the material that has the stronger attraction (the balloon). This causes both materials to become charged. The material losing electrons becomes positively charged and the material gaining electrons becomes negatively charged. The diagram shows that the balloon and hand are electrically neutral before rubbing—that is, each have an equal number of positive and negative charges. After rubbing, the balloon has extra negative charges and the hand is left with extra positive charges. Electric charges follow certain rules, and one rule states that unlike charges are attracted to each other; thus, the negatively charged balloon is attracted to the positively charged hand because of the difference in their charges. Notice in the diagram that there is no change in the total number of combined positive and negative charges on the objects before and after rubbing them together. The rubbing causes the already-present electrons to move from one object to the other.

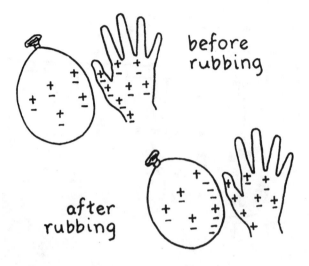

LET'S EXPLORE

1. Does the number of times the balloon is rubbed affect the results? Repeat the experiment twice: first decrease the number of times the balloon is rubbed, and then increase the number of rubbings.

2. Would rubbing the balloon with different materials affect the results? Repeat the original experiment, rubbing the balloon with different types of cloth such as cotton, wool, silk, and/or rayon and with materials such

as paper and plastic. **Science Fair Hint:** Photographs taken during the testing of the materials, the testing materials themselves, and the results of the test can be used as part of a project display.

3. Does the shape of the balloon affect the results? Repeat the original experiment, replacing the round balloon with a long balloon and/or balloons with wavy shapes.

SHOW TIME!

1. Demonstrate that there is an excess of charge on the area where the balloon is rubbed. Use a marker to put an X on the area of the balloon to be rubbed. Repeat the original experiment, giving the balloon a slight spin to cause it to rotate. The balloon will turn and stop with the X facing your hand.

2. Another way to demonstrate static electricity is to lay about 20 pieces of puffed rice cereal on a table. Wad a 2-foot (60-cm) piece of plastic food wrap to form a piece about the size of your fist. Quickly rub the plastic wrap back and forth across a sheet of paper 10 to 15 times. Immediately hold the plastic above the puffed rice. The plastic should be near, but not touching, the cereal.

3. Clothes removed from a clothes dryer often cling to each other. Prepare a display using simple diagrams or photographs to represent common everyday examples of static electricity.

CHECK IT OUT!

Use an encyclopedia, physical science text, and/or other books about electricity to find out more about static electricity. What kind of materials are more likely to be positive? Or negative? How do static charges affect electrical equipment?

4

Zap!

PROBLEM

What happens when static electricity is discharged?

Materials

scissors
ruler
plastic report folder
modeling clay
large paper clip
wool scarf

Procedure

1. Cut a 2-inch × 8-inch (5-cm × 20-cm) strip from the plastic report folder.

2. Use a walnut-sized piece of clay to stand the paper clip upright on a table.

3. Darken the room and wrap the scarf around the plastic strip.

4. Quickly pull the plastic through the scarf. Do this rapidly at least three times.

5. Immediately hold the plastic near, but not touching, the top of the paper clip.

Results

A bright spark of light leaps between the plastic strip and the paper clip.

Why?

Like all atoms, the atoms in the paper clip have a positive center, the nucleus, with negatively-charged electrons spinning around it. Rubbing the plastic against the wool causes some electrons

from the wool to collect on the plastic. This build-up of electrons produces what is called static electricity. These static charges follow the law of electric charges, which states that like charges repel each other and unlike charges attract each other. Holding the negatively-charged plastic near the electrically neutral paper clip causes the negatively-charged electrons in the clip to move

away because of the repulsion between like charges. This creates a positive charge on the surface of the clip near the plastic.

When the charge on the plastic is great enough, the air between the two materials also becomes charged, thereby forming a path through which electrons can move. The resulting spark is called a **static discharge**, which is a loss of static electricity. This discharge can be a very slow, quiet transfer of charges or, as in this experiment, quick with a spark of light and/or a crackle of sound.

LET'S EXPLORE

1. Does the number of strokes of the wool against the plastic affect the results? Repeat the experiment twice, first rubbing the plastic once, and then rubbing the plastic six times.

2. Does the material being charged affect the results? Repeat the original experiment, replacing the plastic strip with materials such as a clean drinking glass and a rubber comb.

SHOW TIME!

1. Lightning is one of the most spectacular displays of static discharge. All of the processes that lead to separation of positive and negative charges in a cloud are not fully understood. Some processes that cause charge separation are the splitting of water drops, the freezing of water or melting of ice, and the rubbing of materials together.

During a thunderstorm, violent air currents move up and down inside the clouds, rubbing water droplets and ice crystals against each other. This movement is but one of the processes that fills the clouds with a charge of static electricity—just as rubbing the plastic and wool together in the original experiment produced a charge.

Find out how the discharge of static charges produces lightning between two clouds and between a cloud and the ground. Use this information to prepare a display chart of the events leading up to a flash. Include steps such as:

- the location of charges in a cloud
- the movement of a "stepped leader"
- upward streams of positive charges
- a stroke of lightning

For more information about lightning, see pages 126–127 in *USA Today: The Weather Book*, by Jack Williams (New York: Vantage Books, 1992).

2a. Demonstrate that the discharge of static electricity produces **radio waves** (energy waves that can travel at the speed of light in a vacuum). This can be done by tuning an AM radio to a position between stations and setting a very low volume. Charge an inflated balloon by rubbing it quickly across a piece of wool about 10 times (or rub the balloon against your clean, dry, oil-free hair). As you hold the balloon near, but not touching, the radio antenna, listen for a single pop that will be heard as the static electricity is discharged from the balloon. For more information about radio waves produced by static discharge, see page 180, "Micro-Bolt," in *Janice VanCleave's Earth Science for Every Kid*, by Janice VanCleave (New York: Wiley, 1991).

b. To see an example of electromagnetic radiation, repeat the previous experiment, this time holding the charged balloon near, but not touching, a paper clip as in the diagram. This works best in a darkened room. The spark of light is a type of electromagnetic radiation.

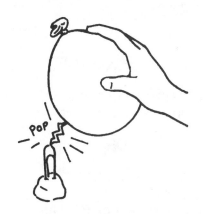

CHECK IT OUT!

According to information found on pages 111–114 in *The Weather Companion*, by Gary Lockhart (New York: Wiley, 1988), lightning is not equally attracted to all trees. Use this book and other resources to discover which trees are more likely to be struck by lightning. What are the characteristics of trees that are more electrically attractive?

5

Glow Bulb

PROBLEM

How can a fluorescent tube glow without being connected to an electric current?

Materials

dishwashing liquid
paper towels
fluorescent tube (size and shape of the
    tube does not matter and it can be a
    burned-out tube)
large bath towel (longer than the
    fluorescent tube)
plastic report folder
adult helper

Procedure

NOTE: This experiment is best performed at night or in a darkened room without windows.

1. Ask an adult to wash and thoroughly dry the outside of the fluorescent tube with paper towels.

2. Stretch out the bath towel near the edge of a table.

3. Lay the fluorescent tube on the bath towel.

4. Darken the room by turning off the lights.

5. Ask your adult helper to rub the plastic folder back and forth across the tube. *CAUTION: Care should be taken not to press too hard, as the tube could break.*

Results

The fluorescent tube starts to glow and the light moves back and forth with the movement of the plastic.

Why?

Rubbing the tube results in a build-up of charges, called static charge, on the outside of the glass. This outside charge attracts charged particles inside the tube. The phosphor powder coating on the inside of the tube gives off light when struck by these charged particles.

LET'S EXPLORE

1. Can other materials produce a static charge on the glass? Repeat the experiment, replacing the plastic report folder with materials such as a piece of plastic food wrap, a wool scarf, and an inflated balloon. **Science Fair Hint:** Record your results in a data

chart similar to the one shown here. Describe the light's intensity as *bright*, *medium*, or *dim*.

STATIC CHARGERS	
Materials	**Light Intensity**
plastic folder	
plastic wrap	
wool cloth	
inflated balloon	

2. Will other types of light bulbs give the same results? Repeat the original experiment, replacing the fluorescent tube with an ordinary filament light bulb.

SHOW TIME!

1. People have not always been able to light up their home by simply flipping a switch. Find out about the history of lamps and lighting. Construct a display chart similar to the one shown here to indicate various steps in the advancement of lighting.

LAMPS & LIGHTING

torches

oil lamps

firefly lanterns

fluorescent lamps

2. The light intensity of all light bulbs is not the same. A simple **photometer** (an instrument used to measure the brightness of a light) can be constructed by sandwiching a piece of aluminum foil between two 5-inch × 2½-inch × ½-inch (12.7-cm × 6.4-cm × 1.3-cm) blocks of paraffin (paraffin can be found where food canning supplies are sold). The dimensions of the blocks are not critical, as long as the blocks are of equal size. Use rubber bands to hold the blocks together. Lay a yardstick (meterstick) on the edge of a table. Take two lamps without shades and place one at each end of the stick. Insert different wattage bulbs in the lamps. Hold the photometer so that the edge points toward you and the flat sides face the lamps. Move the photometer above the measuring stick between the bulbs until the edges of both sides of the photometer look equally bright. At this point, an equal amount of light is entering each side and being reflected by the foil. The photometer will be closer to the bulb with the lesser intensity (lower wattage).

CHECK IT OUT!

1. A fluorescent tube shines brightly and steadily when connected to a constant flow of electricity. Look up *lighting* in different encyclopedias to discover how fluorescent lights work.

2. Thomas Alva Edison produced the first practical incandescent light bulb in 1879. There were many failures before the successful bulb was produced. Find out more about the history of the first electric lights. What role did a whisker from Mr. Edison's assistant and sewing thread from Mrs. Edison's sewing basket play in the development of bulbs that could burn for more than a few hours?

6

Charger

PROBLEM

How can materials be charged without being touched?

Materials

scissors
ruler
aluminum foil, as thin as possible
pencil, well sharpened
needle-nosed pliers
large paper clip
poster board
1-quart (1-liter) glass jar
modeling clay
masking tape
9-inch (23-cm) round balloon
wool scarf
adult helper

Procedure

1. Cut two ½-inch x 2-inch (1.3-cm × 5-cm) strips of foil.

2. Use the pencil point to make a small hole very near one end of each foil strip. Keep the strips smooth and flat.

3. Ask an adult to use the pliers to reshape the paper clip into a loop with two hooks at the bottom, as shown in the diagram.

4. Cut a circle from the poster board to fit over the top of the jar.

5. Ask your adult helper to use the pencil point to make a hole in the center of the paper circle.

6. Push the loop of the wire through the hole in the paper circle. Mold a small piece of clay around the base of the loop to hold the wire in place.

7. Hang the foil strips on the wire hooks. They should jiggle back and forth freely. If they do not, enlarge the hole with the pencil point.

8. Place the paper circle over the mouth of the jar with the foil strips inside the jar.

9. Tape the paper cover onto the mouth of the jar.

10. Inflate the balloon and rub it on the scarf. *NOTE: You can rub the balloon on your hair if it is clean, dry, and oil-free.*

11. Hold the balloon near the loop on top of the jar and then move it away.

Results

The metal strips move apart when the balloon is held near, then hang straight down again when the balloon is removed.

Why?

The instrument made is called an **electroscope**, or static charge detector. The metal strips, which are hanging from the wire hooks, become charged and move away from each other when an electrically-charged object is placed near the top of the wire. In this case, the metal as a whole is still electrically neutral, but the charges are moved around within the metal so that some parts are more positive than negative and other parts are more negative than positive. The charge on parts of an object produced simply by bringing another charged object near with no transfer of charge from one object to the other is called an **induced charge**. In this experiment the balloon was first charged by rubbing electrons from your hair onto the balloon, creating a negative charge on the surface of the balloon. When the charged balloon is held near the top of the metal loop, it produces an induced charge on the metal strips. The negative charge on the balloon repels the negatively-charged electrons on top of the metal loop, causing the electrons in the metal to move away from the balloon and toward the metal strips. These excess electrons in the strips cause them both to become negatively charged. Because like charges repel each other, the two negatively-charged strips move apart. Removing the charged balloon allows the electrons to return to their original positions, which in turn allows the metal strips to return to their original positions. The metal leaves were temporarily charged.

LET'S EXPLORE

1. Touching the charged balloon to the metal loop, rather than just holding it near, allows some of the excess charges on the balloon to move to the metal strips. The strips become charged by **conduction** (charging an uncharged object by touching it with a charged object). Would charging by conduction affect the results of the experiment? Repeat the experiment, but this time allow the charged balloon to touch the metal loop before being removed.

2. If the metal strips remain separated even after the charged balloon is removed, the strips are said to have a **residual charge** (charge retained by an object after the charging body has been removed). Can a residual charge be placed on the strips by **induction** (the process by which an induced charge is placed on an object)? Repeat the original experiment. While the balloon is near the metal loop, ask a helper to touch the metal loop with one finger. Remove the finger from the loop before removing the charged balloon. **Science Fair Hint:** Draw diagrams to represent the results of each experiment. Use the facts that like charges repel each other and unlike charges attract to explain each result.

SHOW TIME!

Objects surrounded by electrical conducting material such as metal are more protected from outside static charges. Test the shielding against static charges by using a paper hole-punch to cut small circles of tissue paper. Place the circles of paper on a table and hold a charged balloon near, but not touching, the paper

pieces. Repeat the procedure twice, first by covering the paper pieces with a wire strainer and holding the charged balloon near, but not touching, the strainer, then by touching the wire strainer with the charged balloon.

CHECK IT OUT!

In 1785, Charles Coulomb, a French physicist, measured the electrostatic force between two like charged objects. In his honor, the unit for measuring electric charges is called the coulomb. Find out more about the *coulomb* unit. One coulomb equals the charge on how many electrons?

7

How High?

PROBLEM

What is voltage?

Materials

2-quart (2-liter) bowl (made of material not easily broken)
2 paper towels
yardstick (meterstick)
raw, uncracked, medium-sized egg
2 helpers

Procedure

1. Line the inside of the bowl with the
paper towels.

2. Place the bowl on the floor.

3. Ask a helper to hold a yardstick (meterstick) upright next to the bowl.
The bottom of the measuring stick
should be on the floor.

4. Hold the egg 12 inches (30 cm) above
the bottom of the bowl.

5. Ask a second helper to be prepared to
observe the egg as it lands in the
bowl.

6. Drop the egg. Do not throw it—just
release it and allow it to fall.

Results

The results can vary depending on the
strength of the egg shell, but typically the
egg will crack and some of its contents
will spill into the bowl.

Why?

When you lifted the egg, you did **work** (using force to move an object). The raised egg has **potential energy** (stored energy) equal to the amount of work needed to lift it. Therefore, the egg has more potential energy at the top than at the bottom of its fall. The energy of the egg simulates the energy of an electron at different places in an **electric circuit** (the path that an electric current

follows). In a **battery** (a device that uses chemicals to produce an electric current) electrons build up at one end. Work was done to cause this. As a result, the electrons have gained potential energy. The end of the battery is a place of high potential energy. The other end of the battery, without a build-up of electrons, is a place of low potential energy. The difference between the potential energy of the two ends is called **potential difference**, or voltage. **Voltage** is measured in **volts** and is the energy available to move charges in a circuit. The higher the voltage, the more energy electrons have, just as the higher the egg, the more energy the egg has.

LET'S EXPLORE

The height of the egg changes the egg's potential energy. Prove this by repeating the experiment twice. First raise the egg to a height of 6 inches (15 cm), and then increase the height to 24 inches (60 cm). **Science Fair Hint:** Display photographs in sequence showing the egg at each height and its effect on the egg when dropped.

SHOW TIME!

1. Another way of describing voltage is by comparing it to the potential energy of water in a cup, which is determined by the height of the cup. You can demonstrate the difference of potential energy due to height by holding a paper cup with a hole in the bottom above a paddle wheel. Make the paddle wheel by gluing stiff paper pieces around a thread spool. Push a pencil through the center hole of the

spool. The pencil must be thin enough to allow the spool to spin around freely. Ask a helper to hold the paddle wheel over a bucket and allow the water to flow out of the cup and onto the paddles. Double the height of the cup above the wheel and observe the difference in its rotation speed.

2. Explain how dropping a tennis ball from different heights into a bowl of water can be compared to the voltage of batteries. *NOTE: Perform this experiment outdoors using a plastic bowl.* Repeat the original experiment twice: first drop the ball from a height of 1 foot (30 cm), and then drop the ball from a height of 2 feet (60 cm).

A single size AA, AAA, C, or D battery, which has a current of 1.5 **V** (the symbol for volt), can be represented by the ball that is dropped from the shorter height. Connecting two 1.5 V batteries, such as in a flashlight, doubles the voltage and gives their electrons 3 V of energy. The combined batteries can be compared to the ball that falls from the higher, doubled, height. Prepare diagrams comparing the energy of the falling ball to the batteries.

CHECK IT OUT!

Voltage can be described as the energy that moves electrical charges between two points. Find out more about this electrical measurement. How was the unit name *volt* derived? What is the voltage of ordinary house current? Ask an adult to assist you in making a survey of the required voltage for some of the appliances in your home. What are *transformers* and why are they so important?

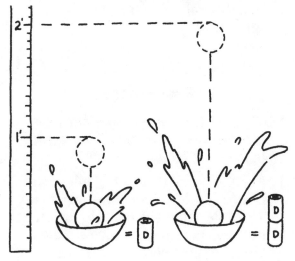

Flow Rate

PROBLEM

How do you measure the flow of electricity?

Materials

pencil
7-oz (210-ml) paper cup
masking tape
7 oz (210 ml) table salt
small bowl
stopwatch
helper

Procedure

NOTE: This experiment works best on a dry day because salt tends to stick together when the air is humid.

1. Use the pencil to punch a hole in the center of the bottom of the paper cup. The hole should be equal to the **circumference** (the distance around a circle) of the pencil.

2. Place a piece of tape over the hole.

3. Fill the cup with salt.

4. Hold the cup of salt about 6 inches (15 cm) above the bowl, and ask your helper to start the stopwatch the second you remove the tape from over the hole in the cup.

5. Tell your helper to stop the stopwatch as soon as the salt stops pouring out the hole.

6. Calculate the flow rate of the salt by using the following equation:

$$\text{Flow rate} = \frac{\text{amount of salt pouring out, ounces (ml)}}{\text{total pouring time, seconds}}$$

Results

The time for the salt to pour from the cup can vary depending on the hole size made by the pencil. See the example for sample flow rate calculations:

Flow Rate Example

	English		Metric
Flow rate =	$\dfrac{7 \text{ ounces}}{35 \text{ seconds}}$	=	$\dfrac{210 \text{ ml}}{35 \text{ seconds}}$
=	$\dfrac{0.2 \text{ ounces}}{1 \text{ second}}$	=	$\dfrac{6 \text{ ml}}{1 \text{ second}}$

Why?

The flow of salt passing through the hole can be described as the quantity of salt that passes a given point divided by the unit of time. In this experiment, 7 ounces (210 ml) of salt pass out of the cup in 35 seconds, so the flow rate is calculated to be 0.2 ounces (6 ml) per second. The flow rate of the salt simulates, but is not an exact model of, an electric current (the flow rate of electric charge), which is the amount of electric charges passing a given point per second. Electric charges are measured in the metric unit of **coulombs**; thus, the flow rate of a current is measured in coulombs per second. The amount of current flowing through a conductor is usually expressed in **amperes** (amps, for short), which is equal to one coulomb per second.

LET'S EXPLORE

1. Does the amount of salt affect the results? Repeat the experiment twice: first fill a cup one fourth full, and then fill a second cup halfway. Be very careful to make the hole size the same in each cup. Use information about electron movement in Chapter 1 to determine if the results can be compared to current flow in shorter and longer pieces of wire of the same circumference.

2a. How would the size of the hole affect the results? Repeat the experiment twice: first make a small hole in the cup by using only the pointed end of the pencil, and then enlarge the hole in the cup by hollowing it out with the pencil.

b. Repeat the previous procedure, recording the information in a data chart similar to the one shown here. Hole size can be recorded as small, medium, or large. **Science Fair Hint:** Display the data chart for the salt experiment along with a chart displaying samples of different **gauges** (measurement of a wire's circumference) of wire and an indication of how the wire's gauge affects the flow rate of an electric current through the wire.

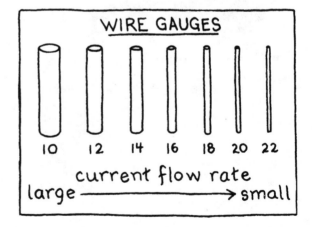

FLOW RATE DATA CHART		
Hole Size	**Time**	**Flow Rate**
small		
medium		
large		

SHOW TIME!

1. Ask an electrician to show you the size of wire coming into a house compared to the size of wire going to electrical outlets and the size of wire going to a lamp. Ask for an explanation about the gauging sizes of wire. Construct a display showing different gauges and uses of wire.

2. Cars on a highway are good models to represent the flow rate of electrons through different gauges of wire. With model cars, arrange a display showing cars lined up on one, two, three, or more laned highways. Use a legend showing that each car represents a single electron and that each size highway indicates a wire gauge. Use your information about wire gauges when comparing highways to wire gauges.

CHECK IT OUT!

The cup of salt contains many individual grains of salt. Instead of counting each grain and determining the flow rate in number of salt grains per unit of time, a larger unit of measurement (cups or ml) was used. Coulomb is a unit used to express a large quantity of electric charges. A current of 1 amp is equal to 1 coulomb of charges per second flowing past a given point. Use a physics book to find out how many electric charges pass a point per second in a 1-amp current.

9

Pathway

PROBLEM

Is aluminum an electrical conductor?

Materials

2 12-inch (30-cm) aluminum foil strips
   (see Appendix)
penny
duct tape
size D battery
2 spring-clip type clothespins
short, wide rubber band
flashlight bulb

Procedure

1. Build a **circuit tester** (an instrument used to test for the flow of electricity) for use in other sections of the book. Follow these steps:

   - Wrap the end of one foil strip around a penny, and tape the foil-wrapped penny to the **negative terminal** (part of the battery from which electrons leave; flat end) of the battery.

   - Open one clothespin and wrap the free end of the foil strip around its tip. Secure the strip to the pin with tape, as in the diagram. This pin will be called the *material holder*.

   - Tape the second foil strip to the **positive terminal** (the part of a battery toward which electrons flow; raised end) of the battery.

   - Place the rubber band around the ends of the battery to securely hold the foil and coin against the battery.

   - Wrap the free end of the foil strip around the base of the flashlight bulb. Be careful not to let the foil strip touch the metal dot on the bottom of the bulb.

- Place the foil-wrapped base of the bulb in the jaws of the second clothespin. This pin will be called the *bulb holder*.

- Lay the foil strip down the side of the bulb holder, and secure with tape.

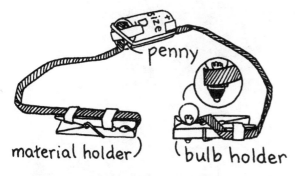

material holder   bulb holder

2. Hold the bulb holder, and press the metal bottom of the bulb against the aluminum strip on top of the *material holder* (the other clothespin).

Results

The bulb glows.

Why?

An electrical conductor, such as aluminum, is a material that allows an electric current to pass through it. Con-ductors, like all matter, are composed of atoms that have a nucleus with positively-charged protons and negatively-charged electrons spinning around the nucleus. Conductors differ from other matter in that they have more electrons called *free electrons* that are free to move through them. When the conductor is connected to a battery, the free electrons are pushed in the same direction. The path through which the electrons move is called an electric circuit. This movement of electric charges is called an electric current, and since the current moves in one direction it is called a **direct current**.

LET'S EXPLORE

1a. Aluminum is a metal. Are other metals conductors? Repeat the experiment using other metals such as a coin made of nickel (a nickel) and an iron nail. Test each metal one at a time by placing one side of the metal in the jaws of the *material holder*. Then press the bulb's metal bottom against the opposite side of the metal being tested.

b. Do materials other than metals conduct an electric current? Repeat the above experiment using materials such as paper, a wooden pencil, and plastic.

2. Would other batteries produce the same results? Repeat the original experiment three times using one of these battery sizes for each experiment: AA, AAA, or C.

3. Electrons move through an electric circuit in wire. The repulsion of the electrons at one end of the wire and their attraction at the opposite end of the wire results in the electrons moving in one direction. Prepare a poster to explain the movement of electrons away from the negative end and toward the positive end of the wire.

SHOW TIME!

Connecting only a single foil strip from the battery to the bulb will not light it. A **closed circuit** (an unbroken current)

foil strip

on off circuit tester

leading from one end of the battery to the other is necessary for the electrons to flow through and cause the bulb to light. The position of the parts of an electrical switch affects whether a circuit is a closed circuit or an **open circuit** (a broken circuit). Make a switch by wrapping the end of an aluminum foil strip around one end of a small paper clip. Make a small hole near the edge of a 4-inch (10-cm) square piece of cardboard. Place the foil-wrapped end of the paper clip over the hole, bend the rest of the foil strip behind the cardboard, and tape it down. Push a paper fastener through the hole, and bend back the ends of the fastener against the cardboard. Make a second hole 1.5 inches (3.8 cm) from the first hole. Push a second paper fastener through and bend back its ends underneath. This fastener will be called the contact point and its ends should not touch the foil or ends of the other fastener. Take the circuit tester from the original experiment and clip the material holder to the cardboard so that the foil strip is in the jaws of the pin. Press the metal bottom of the tester's bulb against the top of the contact point. Rotate the paper clip so that it touches the contact point to switch on the light.

CHECK IT OUT!

If electric charges cannot travel through a material, then that material is a *nonconductor*. Use a physical science text to find out more about conductors and nonconductors. What is an *electrical insulator*?

10

Lemon Power

PROBLEM

How can you make a battery out of a lemon?

Materials

18-gauge copper wire (smaller-gauge
   wire will work)
wire cutters
paper clip
coarse sandpaper
lemon
adult helper

Procedure

1. Ask your adult helper to strip 2 inches
(5 cm) of insulation from the wire.
Cut off the bare metal with the wire
cutters.

2. Then, ask your adult helper to
straighten out the paper clip and cut
a 2-inch (5-cm) piece from one end.

3. Use the sandpaper to smooth any
rough edges from the wire and the
piece of paper clip.

4. Gently squeeze the lemon with your
hands until it feels soft. Do not rup-
ture the lemon.

5. Push the pieces of paper clip and wire
into the lemon so that they are as
close as possible without touching.

6. Moisten your tongue with saliva, and
touch the tip of your wet tongue to the
free ends of the wires.

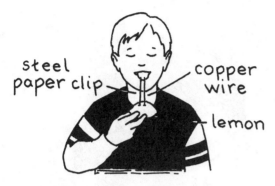

steel paper clip

copper wire

lemon

Results

A slight tingle may be felt and a metallic taste is detected.

Why?

The lemon battery you have created is called a voltaic battery. A voltaic battery, like all batteries, changes chemical energy into electrical energy. It is a battery made up of two different metals called **electrodes** (part of battery where electric current enters or leaves the battery), which are placed in a liquid containing an **electrolyte** (a substance whose water solution can conduct electricity). In a solution of water plus an electrolyte, such as the acid in the lemon, an excess of electrons collects on one of the electrodes, at the same time electrons are lost from the other electrode. Touching the electrodes to your tongue closes the circuit and allows an electric current to flow. The tingle felt and the metallic taste is due to the movement of electrons through the saliva on your tongue.

LET'S EXPLORE

1. Do the types and combinations of metals affect the results? Repeat the experiment using different combinations of metals such as a copper penny and a nickel, or a nickel and a paper clip (steel). Ask an adult to cut slits in the lemon so you can insert the coins. Use new coins or scrub old coins with a dish scouring pad.

2a. Would a different kind of acidic food produce the same results? Repeat the original experiment using other citrus fruits such as grapefruit or oranges. Try noncitrus acidic foods such as tomatoes.

b. Would food not considered to be high in acidic content produce the same results? Repeat the experiment using foods such as bananas or potatoes. **Science Fair Hint:** Photographs along with the results of each experiment can be used as part of a project display.

SHOW TIME!

A single lemon battery will produce about 0.7 volts. If two lemon batteries are connected together, they supply enough voltage to power a digital watch. Build and display a lemon-powered watch by using pennies (copper) and paper clips (steel) as the electrodes. Ask an adult to cut slits in the lemons to hold the electrodes. Insert the penny and paper clip as close as possible in each lemon without touching. Use small flexible wire, such as 22-gauge, and alligator clips to connect the penny in the first lemon to the paper clip in the second lemon. Remove the battery from an inexpensive digital watch. Using two separate 18-gauge wires and alligator clips, connect one wire to the paper clip in the first lemon and the second wire to the penny in the second lemon. Touch the free ends of these two wires to the battery contacts on the watch. To observe the face of the watch, stand it on its side and place a mirror in front of it.

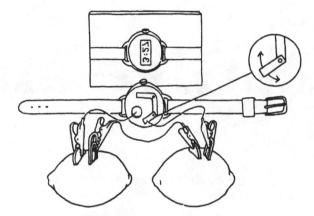

CHECK IT OUT!

In 1792, Alessandro Volta, a professor of physics at the University of Pavia, Italy, discovered that chemical action between two metals could produce electricity. Find out more about Volta's experiments for producing an electric current. One of Volta's most famous experiments—called the *Voltaic pile*—represented the first real electric storage battery. How is a Voltaic pile constructed? Describe Volta's experiment that he called "the crown of cups."

Give and Take

11

PROBLEM

Can an electric current move through water?

Materials

duct tape
3 size D batteries
½ cup (125 ml) of distilled water
cereal bowl (very clean)
12-inch (30-inch) aluminum foil strip
   (see Appendix)
2 clothespins
size D (1½-volt) flashlight bulb
2 helpers (one must be an adult)

Procedure

WARNING: Electricity can be dangerous. Use only 1½-volt batteries—and do not use more than three batteries.

1. Tape the three batteries together with positive terminals touching negative terminals.

2. Pour the distilled water into the bowl.

3. Stand the flat, negative terminal of the battery column in the bowl of water. Ask your adult helper to support the column.

4. Lay one end of the foil strip under the surface of the water in the bowl so that it is near, but not touching, the column of batteries. Hold the strip in position by clipping it to the side of the bowl with a clothespin.

5. Tightly wrap the free end of the foil strip around the metal base of the flashlight bulb. Secure with a clothespin.

6. Squeeze the clothespin tightly against the base of the bulb while pressing the bulb's metal bottom against the raised, positive terminal of the battery column.

7. Ask a second helper to darken the room by closing the window shades and turning off the light.

8. Observe the bulb for about 5 seconds.

WARNING: While the procedure in this experiment is safe, you should not touch this, or any, solution that is connected to an electric current.

Results

The bulb does not glow.

Why?

The flashlight bulb glows only when an electric current flows through its filament. In a circuit, the negative terminal of the connected batteries repels electrons and the positive terminal attracts them, producing a flow of electric charge. However, for electric charges to flow,

there must be a closed circuit which is an unbroken path connecting the bulb and the batteries. Distilled water is not a conductor, so the electric current is interrupted; thus, the bulb does not glow. *WARNING: While it is true that distilled water does not conduct electricity, most water is not distilled so you should never place any electrical appliances in water.*

LET'S EXPLORE

1a. How would adding an electrolyte to the water affect the results? Repeat the experiment by adding 2 teaspoons (10 ml) of table salt to the water in the bowl, and stir until the salt is dissolved. Table salt, like all electrolytes, conducts an electric current when mixed with water. The brightness of the bulb indicates the strength of the current. A large current produces the brightest light. *NOTE: If the bulb does not glow, make sure the foil is wrapped tightly around the bulb and ask your adult helper to press the connected batteries firmly together.*

b. Test other substances to determine whether they are electrolytes or nonelectrolytes. Repeat the previous procedure twice, starting with fresh distilled water in a clean bowl each time. First replace the salt with sugar and then with baking soda. **Science Fair Hint:** Photographs showing the steps of the procedure can be used as part of a project display.

SHOW TIME!

1a. In the previous experiments, electrons do not dive out of the negative end of the battery and swim through a conductive solution to the foil strip connected to the positive terminal of the battery. Instead, electrolytes such as table salt break apart into cations (positive ions) and anions (negative ions). The cations are attracted to the negative terminal of the battery, where they pull off electrons. The anions are attracted to the positive strip, where they give up electrons. Ask a helper to assist in a demonstration to simulate an electric current in an

electrolytic solution (a solution containing an electrolyte). Lay two books on the edge of a table. Leave enough space between the books to line up a row of marbles. The marbles between the books represent the electrons in the electric circuit. Hold a marble in your hand. Your hands represent an anion with an extra electron. Place the marble at the end of the row of marbles. Gently push this marble forward until the marble at the opposite end drops off the table and into your helper's hand. Your helper's hand represents a cation receiving the electron. Observe the movement of each marble.

b. Design a project display poster such as the cartoon diagram shown here to represent the addition of electrons by the anions to the **anode** (positive electrode) and the removal of electrons by the cations at the **cathode** (negative electrode).

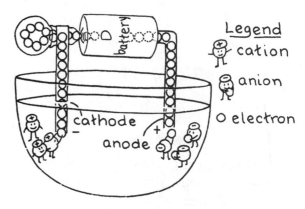

CHECK IT OUT!

The ability of some solutions to conduct an electric current was discovered accidentally by Luigi Galvani, a medical professor, in 1798. Find out more about his experiments, which caused him to believe that within animals there is what he called "animal electricity."

12

Flashlight

PROBLEM

How does a flashlight work?

Materials

flashlight that holds 2 size D batteries
16-inch (40-cm) aluminum foil strip
   (see Appendix)
duct tape
2 size D batteries

Procedure

1. Unscrew the top section (which holds the bulb) from the flashlight.

2. Wrap one end of the foil strip around the base of the bulb holder.

3. Tape the two batteries together with the positive terminal of one touching the negative terminal of the other.

4. Stand the flat, negative terminal of the battery column on the free end of the foil strip.

5. Press the metal tip at the bottom of the flashlight bulb against the positive terminal of the battery, as shown in the diagram.

Results

The light glows.

Why?

The bulb glows when an electric current flows through the circuit, which

includes the battery, foil strip, and fine wire filament inside the flashlight bulb. The movement of the current through the wire filament causes the wire to get hot enough to give off light.

LET'S EXPLORE

1. Does the number of batteries affect the results? Repeat the experiment using only one battery. It is not advis-

able to increase the number of batteries unless you are willing to risk burning out the bulb with excessive current.

WARNING: Other 1½-volt batteries such as size AAA, AA, or C may be used, but do not use more than three 1½-volt batteries. Electricity can be dangerous.

2. Does the size of the flashlight bulb affect the results? The type of bulb a flashlight needs depends on the number of batteries used. Repeat the original experiment using different types of bulbs. Compare and record the illumination of the bulbs as *bright*, *medium*, or *dim*.

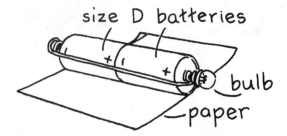

SHOW TIME!

1. Make a model of a flashlight by asking an adult to strip away about 1 inch (2.5 cm) from each end of a 12-inch (30-cm) piece of 18-gauge wire. Wrap about 1 inch (2.5 cm) of one end of the wire around the metal base of a flashlight bulb. Lay two size D batteries on a 4¾-inch (11.9-cm) square piece of paper with the positive terminal of one battery touching the negative terminal of the other. Bend the wire so that the end of the bulb touches the positive terminal of the connected batteries. Lay the rest of the wire along the side of the batteries, with the excess coiled and bent to fit under the negative terminal of the batteries. Wrap the paper tightly around the batteries and wire, and tape the paper together. Stand the batteries on the coiled wire. Make sure the bottom of the bulb is pushed tightly against the top battery and that the coiled end of the wire touches the bottom of the battery.

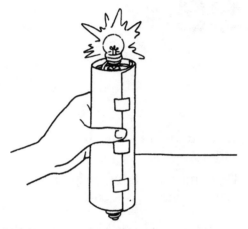

2a. Study different types of flashlights, and make drawings of their parts.

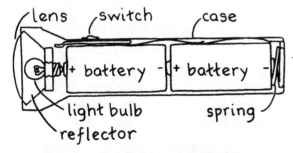

Display the different flashlights along with the drawings.

b. Redesign this homemade flashlight so that it has an "ON/OFF" switch. Display your flashlight models.

CHECK IT OUT!

The shiny metal reflector under the bulb in a flashlight acts like a mirror and has a special shape called a *parabola*. Use a physical science text to find out more about a parabolic mirror. Where and what is the focal point of this mirror, and why is the flashlight bulb placed there?

13

Series

PROBLEM

What is a series circuit and how does it work?

Materials

3 12-inch (30-cm) strips of aluminum
    foil (see Appendix)
new, clean penny
duct tape
size D battery
short, wide rubber band
flashlight bulb
paper clip

Procedure

1. Wrap the end of one foil strip around the penny and tape the foil-wrapped penny to the negative terminal of the battery.

2. Tape the second foil strip to the positive terminal of the battery.

3. Stretch the rubber band around the battery to secure the coin and strips tightly against the battery ends.

4. Twist the third foil strip tightly around the base of the flashlight bulb.

5. Use the paper clip to attach the free end of the third foil strip to the end of the strip that is attached to the negative terminal of the battery.

6. Touch the metal tip on the bottom of the bulb to the foil strip attached to the positive terminal of the battery.

Results

The light bulb should glow. If the bulb does *not* glow, then:

- Check all connections.
- Ask a helper to hold the metal strips tightly against the ends of the battery.
- Be sure the metal tip on the bulb is clean.
- Replace the bulb, which may be burned out.

Why?

When there is only one path for the electric current to follow, the circuit is called a **series circuit**. The arrows in the diagram represent the flow of electricity away from the negative terminal of the battery, through the bulb, and back to the positive terminal of the battery.

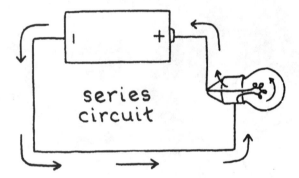

LET'S EXPLORE

1. Would it affect the results if the electricity flows in a reverse direction through the bulb? Repeat the experiment, reversing the positions of the terminals. **Science Fair Hint:** Make a drawing showing the flow of electricity, and indicate whether or not the bulb glows.

2. Can a series circuit have more than one light bulb? Repeat the original experiment using two light bulbs. Connect the bulbs as shown in the diagram so there is only one path for the electric current. **Science Fair Hint:** Create diagrams of the circuits with both one and two bulbs. Indicate the brightness of the bulbs in each circuit.

SHOW TIME!

1. In a flashlight that has two batteries, they are connected in a series by stacking them with the positive terminal of one battery against the negative terminal of the second battery. Demonstrate this by taping two batteries together with opposite-charged terminals touching.

Repeat the original experiment twice using the connected batteries, first using one bulb, and then using two bulbs. *NOTE: Connecting more than two size D batteries in a series may burn out the bulb.*

2a. If two bulbs are connected in a series and one bulb burns out, the electric current will not be able to complete its path and the second bulb will not glow. Demonstrate this by connecting a battery and two bulbs—one good and one burned out—in series. If a burned-out bulb is not available, use a good bulb with masking tape covering the metal tip on the bottom of the bulb.

b. Does it make any difference which bulb, the good one or the burned-out one, is closest to the negative terminal of the battery? Repeat the above experiment, this time switching the position of the bulbs. Photographs can be displayed to represent the results of each series connection.

CHECK IT OUT!

When light bulbs are connected in a series, the current must flow through the first bulb before it can reach the second bulb. Find out more about series circuits. See Experiment 14 for symbols used in drawing electrical diagrams. Then make drawings of these series combinations:
- 1 battery, 1 light bulb, 1 switch.
- 2 batteries, 2 light bulbs, 1 switch.

14

Parallel

PROBLEM

What is a parallel circuit and how does it work?

Materials

4 12-inch (30-cm) strips of
    aluminum foil (see Appendix)
new, clean penny
duct tape
size D battery
short, wide rubber band
2 flashlight bulbs
paper clip
helper

Procedure

1. Wrap the end of one foil strip around the penny, and tape the foil-wrapped penny to the negative terminal of the battery.

2. Tape the second foil strip to the positive terminal of the battery.

3. Stretch the rubber band around the battery to hold the coin and strips tightly against the battery ends.

4. Twist one end of each remaining foil strip tightly around the base of a flashlight bulb.

5. Use the paper clip to attach the free ends of the remaining foil strips to the foil strip attached to the negative terminal end of the battery.

6. Rest the metal tips of the bulbs on the foil strip attached to the positive terminal of the battery.

Results

Both bulbs glow with the same brightness. If either bulb does *not* glow, then:

- Check all connections.
- Ask a helper to hold the metal strips tightly against the ends of the battery.
- Be sure the metal tips on the bulb are clean.

- Replace the bulb that does not glow; it may be burned out.

Why?

When an electric circuit provides more than one path for electric current to follow through, the circuit is called a **parallel circuit**. The characters in the diagram on page 58 represent charges moving through a parallel circuit. The electric current leaves the negative terminal of the battery and arrives at point A, where it separates into two different paths. At point B, the divided current combines again and flows into the positive terminal of the battery. Even though the current divides and takes different paths, the "push" or voltage of the current is the same in each path; thus, the two light bulbs connected in a parallel circuit glow with equal intensity.

LET'S EXPLORE

Would changing the number of light bulbs affect the results? Repeat the experiment several times, increasing the number of bulbs by one each time until there are a total of four to six bulbs all connecting in parallel with each other. Helpers will be needed to assist in hold-

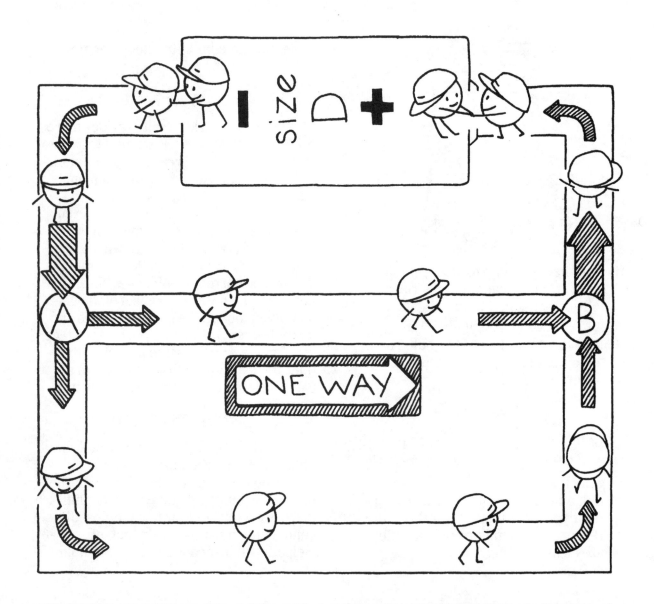

ing the extra bulbs in place. **Science Fair Hint:** Display diagrams and models of the circuits constructed.

SHOW TIME!

1a. When one light in your home or school burns out or is turned off, all of the other lights stay on because they are connected in a parallel circuit. Ask an electrician to help you design and construct a small model of a two- or three-room building using flashlight bulbs for ceiling lights and batteries to provide the power. Switches for the lights and room furnishings will make this an even more presentable project display.

b. Electricians and scientists who study electricity use symbols to draw electric circuits. Some of these symbols, as well as a simple parallel circuit, are shown in the diagram. Use these symbols and others found in a physical science text to make an electrical diagram of the model building. Display the electrical diagram.

CHECK IT OUT!

Conducting metals such as copper, silver, and tantalum are used to print electrical circuits on flat panels, in much the same way as words are printed in ink on the pages of this book. Find out more about printed electrical circuits. One source of information might be a television repair person. Display photographs of a circuit board with an explanation of how it was printed and what it is used for.

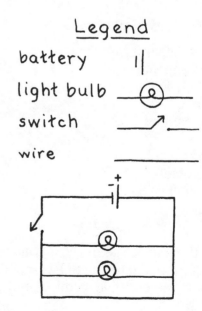

Resistance

PROBLEM

Does the thickness of a wire affect the flow of an electric circuit?

Materials

2 8-inch (20-cm) foil strips
   (see Appendix)
3 new, clean pennies
duct tape
size D battery
short, wide rubber band
flashlight bulb
coarse steel wool
large steel paper clip

Procedure

1. Wrap the end of one foil strip around the penny, and tape the foil-wrapped penny to the negative terminal of the battery.

2. Tape the second foil strip to the positive terminal of the battery.

3. Stretch the rubber band around the battery to hold the coin and strips tightly against the battery ends.

4. Take the free end of the foil strip that is attached to the negative terminal of the battery and twist it tightly around the base of the bulb.

5. Pull a single strand out of the steel wool, and tape one end to the face of a penny.

6. Pull the steel strand taut, and tape its free end to the third penny so that 1 inch (2.5 cm) of the steel strand is stretched between the two coins. Cut off any excess.

7. Touch the bottom of the bulb to one of the coins, and touch the free end of

the foil strip attached to the positive terminal of the battery to the other coin.

8. Observe the brightness of the bulb.

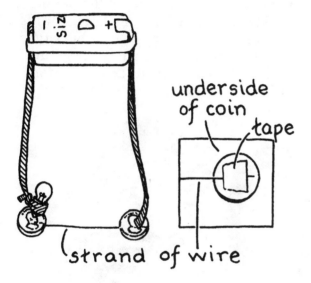

underside of coin

tape

strand of wire

9. Replace the strand of steel wool with a straightened paper clip. Let the ends of the paper clip extend past the coins so that 1 inch (2.5 cm) of the metal lies between the coins.

10. Repeat steps 4 through 7.

Results

The light glows much more brightly with the thicker wire from the paper clip.

Why?

The steel wool strand and the steel paper clip both allow electric current to move through them; thus, both are conductors. The brightness of the bulb indicates that the thicker steel paper-clip wire has more electric current going through it than the thin steel wire. The measure of how difficult it is for an electric current to move through a material is its **electrical resistance**. The thinner the wire, the greater its resistance and the less electric current going through it. The unit of measuring electrical resistance is the **ohm**.

LET'S EXPLORE

1. Does the length of the wire affect the results? Repeat the experiment twice, first using shorter lengths of wire, and then increasing the wire lengths.

2. Does the type of material linking the coins affect the result? Repeat the

previous experiment using different materials such as rubber bands, strands of hair, and copper wire. **Science Fair Hint:** Display the different materials used in each experiment, along with diagrams showing light bulbs and indicating their brightness. Label the materials as low, medium, high, and very high resistance. The materials with very high resistance will be those that completely oppose the flow of electricity so that the bulb does not glow.

SHOW TIME!

1. Simulate the difference in the size of electric currents flowing through wires with different gauges (small and large circumferences). Punch two holes in the side of a paper cup near its bottom. Make one hole the size of the pencil

point and the second hole the circumference of the pencil itself. Hold the cup above a large bowl while a helper pours water into the cup. Observe the size of the water streams pouring out of the two holes. Photographs can be used to represent the results.

2. The gauging of wire indicates its circumference. Use books about electricity and/or ask an electrician to find out how wire gauging and resistance are related. Display samples of wire, placing the wire in order of lowest to highest resistance. Label the gauge for each wire.

3. A more powerful battery or electrical source can force a larger current through any wire. Wires made from metal with high resistance, like nichrome and tungsten, get hotter than wires with low resistance when large electric currents pass through them. Nichrome is used in toasters and tungsten is used to make the filament in light bulbs. When a large current passes through either of these two metals, they get hot. The nichrome gets hot enough to toast bread, and the tungsten gets so hot that it glows. Make a

survey of the electrical appliances in your home to learn which contain electrical wires that get hot due to resistance. Display diagrams or photographs of these items with an explanation of why they heat up.

ELECTRICAL APPLIANCES

toaster: ═══════

light bulb: ═══════

hair dryer: ═══════

CHECK IT OUT!

As the temperature of a metal wire decreases, its resistance also decreases. Find out more about the effect of temperature on the resistance in metals. Can metals get cold enough to lose all electrical resistance? What are *superconductors*? At what temperature does mercury become a superconductor? What are some uses for superconductors?

16

Protectors

PROBLEM

How do fuses protect wires from over-heating?

Materials

2 16-inch (40 cm) foil strips (see Appendix)
2 clothespins
duct tape
medium-grade steel wool pad without soap (found with painting supplies)
large dinner plate
2 size D batteries (works best if new)

Procedure

1. Insert the end of one foil strip into the jaws of one clothespin. Lay the strip across the top of the pin and secure with tape, as in the diagram. Repeat this procedure using the second foil strip and clothespin.

2. Pull a single strand of wire from the steel wool pad.

3. Stretch the strand of wire between the jaws of the clothespins. They should be as close as possible without touching.

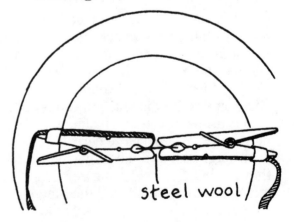

steel wool

4. Place the clothespins on the plate, turning them so that they are on their sides, and the foil strip on one pin is at the top and the foil strip on the second pin is at the bottom, as in the diagram.

5. Tape the two batteries together so that the positive terminal of one battery touches the negative terminal of the other.

6. Dim the lights in the room. While looking down at the strand of wire, touch the ends of the foil strips to the terminals of the battery column.

7. The results will be observed in less than 5 seconds. Immediately remove the strips from the battery terminal. *WARNING: Holding the foil against the battery terminals for longer than 10 seconds can cause them to get hot and burn your fingers.*

Results

The strand of wire glows brightly, then breaks.

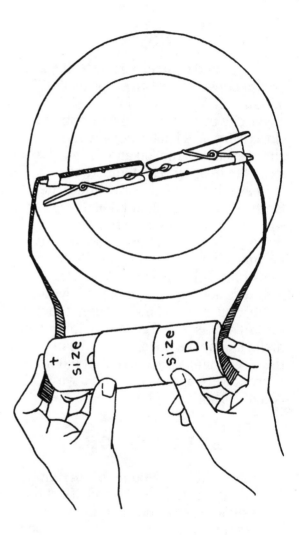

Why?

The strand of steel wool acts like a bridge between the two strips of aluminum foil. With the bridge in place, electricity current can flow through the closed circuit. This flow of electric charges causes the foil and the steel wool strand to heat up. The temperature increase does not appear to affect the larger strips of aluminum foil. However, when a large enough current flows through the circuit, the strand of wire becomes hot enough to melt. In this way, the strand behaves like an electrical fuse. A **fuse** is a safety device that allows an electric current to flow through it, but if the current is too large, a wire in the fuse melts and opens the circuit. This break in the circuit stops the current. If too much current were to pass through a wire, it could get hot enough to cause a fire.

LET'S EXPLORE

1. How would the amount of current flowing through the strand affect the results? Repeat the experiment twice. First use one battery, and then repeat again using three batteries. As the number of batteries increases, the amount of current pushed through the wire also increases.

2. Would the size of the steel wool strand affect the results? Repeat the original experiment twice. First use fine-grade steel wool, and then use coarse-grade steel wool. Use information from Experiment 15 to relate strand size to resistance of current flow.

SHOW TIME!

Circuit breakers (switches that automatically open an electric circuit when too much current is flowing) have replaced fuses in most modern homes. One example of this electrical protector has a switch made of two strips of dissimilar metal bonded together. When the bimetal strip is cool, it lays flat and bridges the gap between two points. If the strip heats up from an excessive flow of electricity, the metal on one side expands more than the metal on the other side. This causes the bimetal strip to curve, with the more-expanded metal forming the outside of the curve. When the strip curves, so that it no longer lays flat enough to form a bridge, electricity

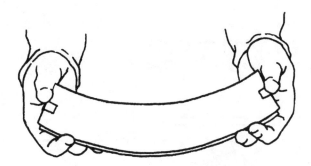

cannot flow through it. Simulate the curving of the bimetal strip by cutting one 2-inch × 8-inch (5-cm × 20-cm) strip and one 2-inch × 8 ¼-inch (5-cm × 21-cm) strip from poster board. Attach them at both ends with tape. Then, while holding both ends, push one side gently. The strip curves toward the side with the shorter piece.

CHECK IT OUT!

1. Grounding is another way of preventing shocks and protecting appliances. Use an encyclopedia or ask an electrician to find out more about this practice. Explain why water pipe systems or metal rods driven into the earth are excellent grounding devices.

2. In 1746, Benjamin Franklin invented the lightning rod. Find out more about how this device protects buildings from lightning, which can produce a giant electric spark carrying up to several million volts. The electricity in your home ranges from 120 to 220 volts. Why is a lightning rod pointed on its top? What happens when lightning strikes the rod?

17

Attractive

PROBLEM

Can electricity produce a magnet?

Materials

wire cutter
1 yard (1 m) 18-gauge wire
16D iron nail
2 pencils
sheet of typing paper
duct tape
2 size D batteries
iron filings (found in inexpensive mag-
    netic drawing toys sold at toy stores
    or teacher supply stores)
adult helper

Procedure

1. Ask an adult to use the wire cutters to strip 2 inches (5 cm) of insulation from both ends of the wire.

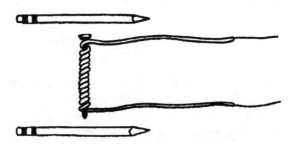

2. Wrap the insulated part of the wire tightly around the nail, leaving about 6 inches (15 cm) of wire on each end.

3. Lay the wrapped nail on a *wooden* table and lay both pencils perpendicular to the nail, one at each end.

4. Cover the nail and pencils with the sheet of typing paper.

5. Tape the two batteries together with the positive terminal of one touching the negative terminal of the other.

6. Touch the free ends of the wire to the terminals of the connected batteries, one to each end.

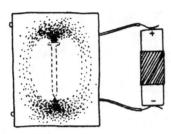

7. While the wires are touching the battery terminals, ask your helper to sprinkle iron filings on the paper above the nail. Tap the paper gently to help the pattern form. *WARNING: DO NOT hold wire against battery terminals longer than 10 seconds. They can get hot and burn your fingers.*

Results

The iron filings form a pattern of lines around the nail.

Why?

All wires carrying a direct current are surrounded by a steady **magnetic field** (the area in which **magnetic force**—the push or pull around a magnet—can be detected). When an electric current flows through a coil of wire, the whole coil acts like a magnet. This type of mag-

net is called an **electromagnet**. Winding the wire into a coil increases the strength of the magnetic field around the electromagnet. The iron nail becomes magnetized by the magnetic field around the wire, adding to the strength of the electromagnet. The iron filings are attracted by the electromagnet and they line up in the direction of its magnetic force field, forming a pattern.

LET'S EXPLORE

1. Would the amount of current flow affect the results? Repeat the experiment twice: first use one battery, and then use three batteries. As the number of batteries increases, the amount of current pushed through the wire increases.

2. Does the number of times the wire is wrapped around the nail affect the results? Repeat the original experiment twice: first use a wire 1.5 feet (45 cm) long, and then use a wire 6 feet long (2 m). The longer wire may require that you neatly overlap the layers on the nail. Be sure to wrap all the wire in the same direction. **Science Fair**

Hint: A print of the iron filings pattern can be made by spraying a fine mist of white vinegar over the iron filings on the paper. Leave the paper undisturbed for several hours to allow the iron to rust. Turn the paper over and brush the rusty filings into the trash. The rusty marks leave a pattern of the magnetic field on the paper, which can be displayed as part of your project.

3. Does the size of the core that the wire is wrapped around affect the results? Repeat the original experiment twice, first using a smaller nail, then using a larger nail.

SHOW TIME!

1a. Demonstrate the strength of an electromagnet. Create the electro-magnet made in the original experiment using one battery. Use a piece of clay to stand a ruler on a table. Place a saucer filled with BBs next to the ruler. Hold the wire-wrapped nail near and parallel with the ruler, and slowly lower it until BBs move upward and cling to the nail tip. Determine the number of BBs that the electromagnet can lift from different heights.

b. Compare the strengths of different electromagnets. Repeat the previous experiment twice: first use a wire ½ yard (.5 m) long, and then use a wire 2 yards (2 m) long. As in the previous experiment, neatly overlap the excess wire and wrap it all in the same direction. Use a data

Data Chart			
Wire Length	**Number of Times Wrapped**	**Distance**	**Number of BBs**
½ yard (.5 m)			
1 yard (1 m)			
2 yards (2 m)			

CHECK IT OUT!

A coil of wire in a spiral form through which electricity flows is called a *solenoid*. Direct, or DC, current flowing through a solenoid produces an electromagnet. Find out more about electromagnets. Would an electromagnet be produced if alternating, or AC, current flowed through a solenoid? What are some of the uses of electromagnets?

chart similar to the one shown here to record the wire length, the number of times the wire is wrapped around the nail, the distance of the nail tip away from the saucer, and the number of BBs picked up.

18

Pointer

PROBLEM

Does an electric current affect a compass?

Materials

36 inch (1-m) aluminum foil strip
  (see Appendix)
small cereal bowl
sewing needle
bar magnet
tap water
corrugated cardboard
compass
size D battery
adult helper

Procedure

NOTE: Never touch a compass with a magnet. This can change the polarity of the compass needle, causing all directions to be reversed.

1. Wrap the aluminum strip around the bowl as many times as possible, leaving about 6 inches (15 cm) free on both ends of the strip. The first layer should go over the top of the bowl.

2. Magnetize the needle by laying it on the magnet for two minutes.

3. Fill the bowl ¾ full with water.

4. Measure and cut a ¾-inch × ¾-inch (1.9-cm × 1.9-cm) cardboard piece.

5. Ask an adult helper to insert the pointed end of the magnetized needle into the middle of one end of the cardboard square and push the needle through the square until it pokes out of the opposite end. Leave equal lengths of the needle extending from each side of the cardboard.

6. Float the cardboard square gently on the surface of the water, and allow it to come to rest.

7. Use the compass to determine in which direction the ends of the floating needle are pointing.

8. Turn the bowl so that the aluminum strips are running in the same direction as the needle, north to south.

9. Stand the flat, negative terminal of the battery on one of the foil strips.

10. Watch the needle as you touch the free end of the foil strip to the positive terminal of the battery. Remove it from the positive terminal and repeat this step several times.

Results

The floating needle rotates away from its original position when both ends of the metal coil touch the battery, and then returns when one of the ends is removed from the battery.

Why?

The magnetized needle acts like a compass needle, with one end pointing toward the magnetic north pole of the earth. An electric current flows through the coiled strip when it is attached to the battery terminals. Since the aluminum coil is turned in a north-to-south direction, the movement of electrons through the coil produces a magnetic field pointing east and west. The needle is pulled out of position by the attraction of this magnetic field. Disconnecting one end of the coil from the battery stops the current flow. Without the magnetic field around the strip, the needle again lines up with the earth's magnetic field.

LET'S EXPLORE

1. Does the number of windings of the foil strip affect the results? Repeat the experiment twice: first wrap the foil fewer times around the bowl, and then wrap the foil more times around the bowl. Make sure the windings are smooth and lying in the same direction. Compare the speed at which the needle moves each time.

2. Does the direction of the current affect the results? Repeat the original experiment twice: first reverse the battery connections, and then repeat again reversing the direction the foil is wound around the bowl. **Science Fair Hint:** Draw diagrams showing the movement of current from the negative end of the battery to the positive end. Indicate the direction that the needle turns.

3. Would separating the foil affect the results? Repeat the original experiment twice: first cover the aluminum foil with masking tape, and then repeat using insulated 18-gauge or smaller wire instead of the foil strip. Be sure to wind the foil and the wire the same number of times.

SHOW TIME!

1a. Since an electric current produces a magnetic field, could an electric current be used to magnetize a needle? Measure and cut a ¾-inch × ¾-inch (1.9-cm × 1.9-cm) piece of cardboard, and ask an adult to insert a nonmagnetic needle through the cardboard square. Place the cardboard and needle in the center of a 12-inch (30-cm) foil strip, with the needle laying perpendicular to the strip. Lay the strip on a *wooden* table, and stand the battery on one end of the strip. Fold the strip over the needle and hold its ends against the ends of the battery for five seconds. Determine if the needle has been magnetized by placing the cardboard square in a bowl of water. Use a compass to verify that the needle floats in a north to south direction and returns to this position if rotated.

b. Would winding the foil around the needle more times affect the magnetic strength of the needle? Use a 24-inch (60-cm) foil strip. Make three loops in the foil. Place a second square of cardboard with an unmagnetized needle inside the coil. Then, repeat the previous experiment. Compare the strength of the magnetized needles by turning them in an east-to-west position and observing the time it takes for them to return to a north-to-south position.

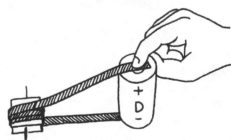

c. Experiment further by using 18-gauge or smaller wire instead of the aluminum foil. Display models of each instrument, indicating the strength of the magnets produced.

19

Jerker

PROBLEM

How does a magnet produce movement in a current-carrying wire?

Materials

2 small disk magnets
duct tape
16-inch (45-cm) wire (18-gauge with
  no insulation)
pencil
size D battery
adult helper

Procedure

1. Place the magnets on the edge of a *wooden* table, leaving a space of about ⅜ inch (1 cm) between them. Make sure oppositely attracting magnetic poles (north and south) face each other.

2. Tape the magnets to the table.

3. Wrap the ends of the wire around a pencil, creating a loop and leaving about 4 inches (10 cm) at either end, as shown in the diagram.

4. Tape the wire to the pencil so that the ends are 2 inches (5 cm) apart.

5. Place the pencil on the table so that the loop is centered between the magnets. Tape the pencil to the table.

6. Observe any movement in the wire loop as you simultaneously touch one

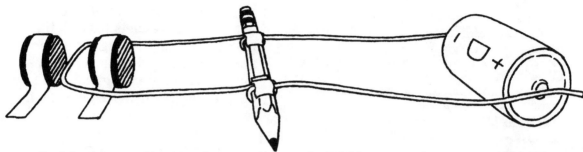

end of the wire to the negative terminal of the battery and the other end of the wire to the positive terminal of the battery.

7. Immediately remove the wire from the battery.

Results

The wire loop jerks either up or down.

Why?

When an electrical current flows through a conductor, such as copper wire, a magnetic field is produced around the wire. If the current-carrying wire is placed in a magnetic field such as between the north and south poles of two magnets, the two magnetic fields oppose each other. The result is a force that tends to expel the wire out of the magnet-

ic field between the two magnets. This movement is known as the **motor effect**.

LET'S EXPLORE

1. Does the direction of the current affect the results? Repeat the experiment, this time reversing the direction of the battery terminals. **Science Fair Hint:** Electrons flow from the negative terminal end of the battery, through the wire, and back to the positive terminal of the battery. Draw diagrams showing the direction of the current. Label the diagram with the words UP or DOWN to indicate the movement of the wire. Include a legend for each part of the diagram, as shown in the figure on the next page.

2. What effect does the strength of the battery have on the results? Repeat

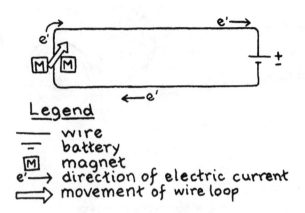

Legend
— wire
= battery
Ⓜ magnet
e'→ direction of electric current
⇒ movement of wire loop

3. What effect does the distance between the magnets have on the results? Repeat the original experiment twice, first increasing the distance between the magnets, and then decreasing the distance between the magnets.

SHOW TIME!

In the original experiment the north pole of one magnet facing the south pole of the second magnet. Construct an instrument that identifies the poles of the magnets by following these steps:

• Cut an L shape from a piece of stiff paper such as poster board. See the diagram for dimensions and labeling.

the original experiment using two batteries. Use tape to connect the positive terminal of one battery against the negative terminal of the other battery.

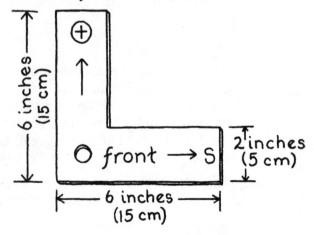

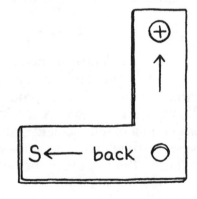

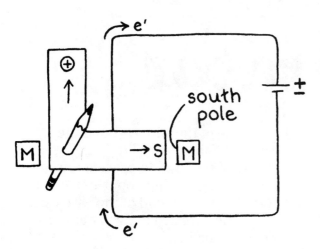

ment of the wire. The pencil should point in the direction that the wire jerks— either up or down. Rotate the instrument so the plus (+) sign lines up with the wire leading toward the positive terminal of the battery. The S on the instrument points toward the magnet, with its south pole facing the wire. The diagram shows the wire jerking up and the south pole of the magnet being identified.

CHECK IT OUT!

Hans Christian Oersted (1777-1851), a Danish scientist, made a very important discovery while giving a lecture demonstration in 1820. Find out more about Oersted and the experiment that proved that an electrical current moving through a wire produces magnetism. You may wish to repeat Oersted's experiment and display diagrams of its results.

- Make a hole in the elbow of the L with a paper hole-punch.
- With the L facing up, insert the pencil point through the hole.

Hold the instrument over one of the diagrams showing current flow and move-

Generator

PROBLEM

Can a magnet produce an electric current?

Materials

wire cutters
ruler
2 7-yard (7-m) pieces of insulated
   20-gauge or smaller wire
duct tape
quart (liter) jar
baby-food jar
compass
modeling clay
bar magnet
adult helper

Procedure

1. Ask an adult to use the wire cutters to strip about 4 inches (10 cm) of insulation from the ends of each piece of wire.

2. Coil one of the wires around the mouth of the quart (liter) jar. Twist the wire together to prevent it from unwinding, leaving about 18 inches (45 cm) of each end of the wire free. Tape the wire coil to the jar to prevent it from slipping.

3. Coil the second wire around the mouth of the baby-food jar. Twist the wire together, leaving about 18 inches (45 cm) of each end of the wire free. Secure with tape.

4. Place the larger jar on its side on a *wooden* table.

5. Twist the bare wire from one jar to the bare wire from the other jar, forming two separated connections.

6. Secure the compass inside the mouth of the larger jar with a small mound of clay.

7. Turn the jar until the coils of wire line up with the compass needle, which points north. Use a small mound of clay to secure the jar to the table so that it does not move.

8. Place the small jar as far apart as possible from the large jar.

9. Ask a helper to dip one end of the magnet in and out of the mouth of the small jar while you watch the compass needle.

Results

The compass needle moves back and forth when the magnet is moved in and out of the jar.

Why?

The movement of a magnet inside the coils of wire generates an electric current. The electric current flows though the wire in one direction when the magnet is pushed into the coil, and in the opposite direction when the magnet is pulled out of the coil. This back and forth movement of an electric current in a conductor is called an **alternating current**. Since a magnetic field is produced around a current carrying wire, the magnetic field around the coil of wire circling the compass is what causes the compass needle to be deflected. The alternating current results in a change in the direction of the magnetic field around the

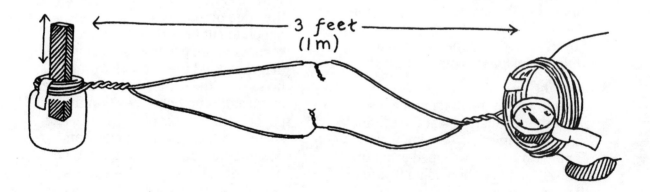

wire, which results in the back-and-forth movement of the needle.

LET'S EXPLORE

1. Does the strength of the magnet affect the amount of energy produced? Use a stronger magnet or make one by stacking round magnets with holes in their centers. Stick a pencil in the hole through the center of the magnets, and secure it with a piece of clay at the bottom of the stack. Hold the pencil to lower and raise the stack of magnets into the jar.

2. Does changing the speed of the moving magnet affect the results? Repeat the original experiment, this time comparing the deflection of the compass needle when the magnet is moved slowly with the deflection when the magnet is moved quickly.

3. Does the number of loops of wire through which the magnet moves affect the results? Repeat the original experiment twice, first using 5 yards (5 meters) of wire wrapped around the large jar, and then using 9 yards (9 meters) of wire.

SHOW TIME!

1. A **generator** is a device that produces electric current by spinning a coil within a magnetic field. Similar results can be achieved by moving a coil back and forth across a magnetic field. Design a method of changing the original experiment so that one of the coils is moved back and forth across the areas between the north and south poles of two magnets.

2. Demonstrate how windmills turn coils in generators by cutting a 6-inch × 6-inch (15-cm × 15-cm) square from a sheet of typing paper. Draw two diagonal lines across the paper and use a coin to draw a circle in the center. With scissors, cut the four lines up to the edge of the circle. Use a paper punch to cut holes in the center and corners of the paper as shown in the diagram. Fold the corners with the holes over the center hole. Push a pencil through the holes, position the paper in the center of the pencil, and secure with clay. Cut a circle from poster board and ask an adult to push the point of the pencil through its center. Lay the pencil in "V's" formed

cut only to here

between your index fingers and thumbs. Blow toward the paper. The turning circle represents turning coils. Use this windmill model to demonstrate the use of wind to generate electric energy.

CHECK IT OUT!

The electric generator was invented by Michael Faraday (1791–1867), an English scientist. Find out more about generators. How do they work? What are they used for?

Aluminum Foil Strips

PURPOSE

To make strips of aluminum foil that can be used to form electrical circuits in this book's experiments.

Materials

ruler
scissors
aluminum foil

Procedure

1. Measure and cut a piece of aluminum foil 2 inches (5 cm) wide and as long as needed for the experiment.

2. Fold the strip in half lengthwise three times to form a thin strip ¼ inch wide.

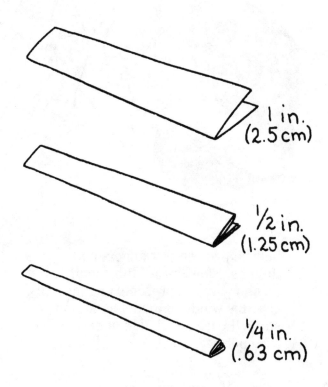

1 in.
(2.5 cm)

½ in.
(1.25 cm)

¼ in.
(.63 cm)

Glossary

Alternating current Back and forth movements of an electric current in a conductor.

Ampere The unit for measuring electric current; amp, for short.

Anion A negatively charged ion; formed when an atom gains one or more electrons.

Anode Positively-charged electrode.

Atom The smallest part of an element that retains the properties of the element; electrically neutral because it has the same number of positive charges (protons), and negative charges (electrons). The protons are in the atom's nucleus and the electrons spin around the outside of the nucleus.

Battery A device that uses chemicals to produce an electric current.

Cathode Negatively-charged electrode.

Cation A positively-charged ion; formed when an atom loses one or more electrons.

Circuit breaker A switch that automatically interrupts or opens an electric circuit when too much current is flowing.

Circuit tester An instrument used to test for the flow of electricity.

Circumference The distance around a circle.

Closed circuit An unbroken circuit; unbroken path of conductors through which an electric current flows.

Conduction, charged by Charging an uncharged object by touching it with a charged object.

Conductor See Electrical conductor.

Coulomb The unit for measuring electric charges.

Diameter The measure of a line crossing a circle and passing through the circle's center point.

Direct current Electrical current that moves in one direction through a circuit.

Electric charge There are only two known types of electric charges, positive and negative. A proton has a positive charge, and an electron has a negative charge.

Electric circuit The path that an electric current follows; a loop of conductors forms the path.

Electric current A flow rate of electric charges; the strength of the current is equal to the amount of electric charges passing a given point per second; measured in amperes.

Electrical conductor A material that allows electric charges to pass through it; usually contain large numbers of electrons called "free" electrons.

Electrical impulse The transfer of electrical energy from one free electron to the next.

Electrical resistance A measure of the difficulty an electric current has in moving through a material; measured in ohms.

Electrically neutral Zero charge; atoms that have an equal number of protons and electrons.

Electricity A form of energy associated with the presence and movement of electrical charges.

Electrode Part of the battery where electric current enters or leaves the battery.

Electrolyte A substance whose water solution conducts an electric current.

Electrolytic solution A water solution containing an electrolyte.

Electromagnet A magnet produced because of the flow of an electric current though a wire; usually made by surrounding an iron core with a coil of wire.

Electron Negatively charged particle moving outside the nucleus of an atom.

Electroscope An instrument used to detect the presence of static charges.

Electrostatic force The force of attraction or repulsion between electric charges.

"Free" electron Electron that breaks away from an atom and wanders around amongst the surrounding atoms within the material.

Fuse A safety device that allows an electric current to flow though it, but if the current is too large, a wire in the fuse melts and opens the circuit. This break in the circuit stops the current.

Gauge The measurement of a wire's circumference; the larger the gauge the smaller the circumference and the smaller the electric current that can pass through.

Generator A device that converts mechanical energy into electrical energy.

Induced charge The charge on an object produced simply by bringing it near another charged object with no transfer of charge from one object to the other; the object as a whole is still neutral, but the charges are moved around within the object so that some parts have a build up of positive charges and other parts have a build up of negative charges.

Induction Process by which an induced charge is placed on an object.

Ion A charged particle produced when an atom gains or loses electrons.

Law of electric charges States that unlike charges attract each other and like charges repel each other.

Magnetic field The area around a magnet in which magnetic forces can be detected.

Magnetic force The push or pull around a magnet.

Matter All the material in the universe. Anything that takes up space and has mass.

Motor effect Motion as a result of placing a current carrying wire in a magnetic field.

Negative terminal The part of a battery from which electrons leave; flat end of a battery.

Neutral See Electrically neutral.

Nucleus The central area of an atom containing positively-charged protons; zero-charged neutrons are also found in this area.

Ohm Unit used to measure electrical resistance.

Open circuit A broken circuit; a break in the path of an electric circuit.

Parallel circuit An electrical circuit that provides more than one path for the electricity to follow.

Photometer An instrument used to measure the brightness of a light.

Positive terminal The part of a battery towards which electrons flow; raised end of a battery.

Potential difference The difference in the potential energy between electrons in one place and electrons in another place; voltage.

Potential energy Stored energy.

Proton Positively-charged particle found inside the nucleus of an atom.

Radio waves Energy waves that can travel at the speed of light in a vacuum.

Repel To push apart from each other, such as like charges.

Residual charge A charge that remains on an object after the charging body has been removed.

Series circuit An electrical circuit that provides only one path for an electric current to follow.

Static charge Stationary electric charges.

Static discharge The loss of static charges.

Static electricity The buildup of static charges in one place; these electric charges can be positive or negative; effects caused by static charges.

Stationary Not moving; remaining in the same place.

Terminal See Negative terminal or Positive terminal.

V The symbol for volt.

Volt Unit of potential difference.

Voltage Potential difference; the energy available to move charges from one point to another in an electric circuit.

Work The use of force to move an object.

Index

ampere, 34
anion:
    definition of, 6, 46
    model of, 6
anode (See electrode)
atoms, 4–7, 13, 16, 37
    definition of, 5
    model of, 4
battery:
    definition of, 30
    electrode, 41, 43
    electrolyte, 41
    lemon, 40–43
    negative terminal of, 36, 45, 46, 54, 57
    positive terminal of, 36, 45, 46, 54, 57
    voltaic, 40–43
cathode (See electrode)
cation:
    definition of, 6, 46
    model of, 6
circuit breaker, 66
circuit tester, 36–39
conduction, charged by:
    definition of, 26
coulomb, 27, 34, 35
Coulomb, Charles, 27
Edison, Alva, 23
electric charges:
    definition of, 5
    unit of, 34
electric circuit:
    closed, 39, 46
    definition of, 29, 37
    diagrams, 59
    open, 39, 66
    parallel, 56–59
    series, 52–55

electric current:
    alternating, 81
    definition of, 7, 29, 33
    direct, 37
    in electrolytic solutions, 46–47
    magnetic field around, 72–75, 81, 77
    produced by a magnet, 80–83
    size of, 62–63
    unit of, 34
    in water, 44–47
electrical conductor, 7, 27, 36–39, 46, 61, 77
    definition of, 7, 37
electrical impulse:
    definition of, 7
    model of, 7
electrical resistance, 60–63
    definition of, 61
    unit of, 61
electrically neutral, 5
electricity:
    definition of, 9
    flow of, 32–35
    movement produced by, 8–11
    static, 12–19
electrode:
    anode, 47
    cathode, 47
    definition of, 41
electrolyte, 41, 46
electrolytic solution, 47
electromagnetic, 68–75
    definition of, 69
    magnetic field of, 69
    strength of, 70–71
electromagnetic radiation, 19
electron:
    definition of, 5

gain of, 6, 14
loss of, 6, 14
movement of, 6–7
electroscope, 24–27
definition of, 26
electrostatic force, 10
Faraday, Michael, 83
flashlight, 48–51
Franklin, Benjamin, 67
"free" electrons, 7, 37
fuse, 64–67
definition of, 66
Galvani, Luigi, 47
generator:
definition of, 82
model of, 82–83
induced charge, 26
induction, 27
ion:
definition of, 5
model of, 6
law of electric charges, 9, 11, 17
light bulbs:
fluorescent, 20–22
glow of, 44–46, 48–51
history of, 22
light intensity of, 22, 23
lightning, 18
magnetic field, 69, 81
definition of, 69
magnetic force, 69
model of, 69
matter:
conductors, 37
definition of, 5
electrical charging of, 4–7

motor effect, 76–79
definition of, 77
model of, 77
nucleus, 5, 9, 37
definition of, 5
Oersted, Christian, 79
ohm, 61
parallel circuit, 56–59
definition of, 57
photometer, 23
potential difference:
definition of, 30
models of, 28–31
potential energy:
definition of, 29
models of, 28–31
proton, 5, 6, 9, 13, 37
radio waves, 19
residual charge, 27
series circuit, 52–55
definition of, 54
static charges, 13, 17, 21
static discharge, 17
static electricity:
definition of, 13, 17
discharge of, 16–19
production of, 12–15
switch, 39
Volta, Alessandro, 43
voltage, 28–31, 57
definition of, 30, 31
models of, 28–31
unit of, 30
wire gauge, 34, 62, 63
defintion of, 34
work, 29, 30

HAVE MORE FUN WITH SCIENCE...
JOIN THE SCIENCE FOR EVERY KID CLUB!

Just fill in the coupon below and mail to:
FAN CLUB HEADQUARTERS/F. Nachbaur
John Wiley & Sons, Inc., 605 Third Avenue, New York, NY 10158

Name_____
Address_____
City_____ State_____ ZIP_____

Membership in the Science for Every Kid Club entitles you to a quarterly newsletter featuring science tidbits, games, and other experiments, plus other surprises...and it's free!!!

✂ —

More Exciting and Fun Activity Books from Janice VanCleave...

Available from your local bookstore or use order form below.

__ ANIMALS (55052-3), @ $9.95
__ EARTHQUAKES (57107-5), @ $9.95
__ GRAVITY (55050-7), @ $9.95
__ MACHINES (57108-3), @ $9.95
__ MAGNETS (57106-7), @ $9.95

To Order by Phone:

__ MICROSCOPES (58956-X), @ $9.95
__ MOLECULES (55054-X), @ $9.95
__ VOLCANOES (30811-0), @ $9.95
__ ASTRONOMY FOR EVERY KID (53573-7), @ $10.95
__ BIOLOGY FOR EVERY KID (50381-9), @ $10.95
__ CHEMISTRY FOR EVERY KID (62085-8), @ $10.95
__ DINOSAURS FOR EVERY KID (30812-9), @ $10.95

Call Toll-Free
1-800-CALL-WILEY

__ EARTH SCIENCE FOR EVERY KID (53010-7), @ $10.95
__ GEOGRAPHY FOR EVERY KID (59842-9), @ $10.95
__ MATH FOR EVERY KID (54265-2), @ $10.95
__ PHYSICS FOR EVERY KID (52505-7), @ $10.95
__ 200 GOOEY, SLIPPERY, SLIMY, WEIRD,
   AND FUN EXPERIMENTS (57921-1), @ $12.95

❑ Payment enclosed (Wiley pays postage & handling)
❑ Charge my ___ Visa ___ Mastercard ___ AMEX
Card # _____ Exp. Date ___/___

Name_____
Address_____
City/State/ZIP_____
Signature_____
(Order invalid unless signed)